Campin

INTRODUCTION

Get away from home, enjoy the fresh air in the countryside or at the beach by going camping! Whether you like a small tent, a large family sized one or something unusual like a Pod, there is plenty of choice. Load up the car with all your equipment and gadgets and with electrical hook-ups available at many sites you can take a portable fridge and recharge your electronic devices. You don't have to spend a lot of money to go camping and it is a lot of fun. You can travel anywhere in the UK or abroad, so enjoy the beach and seaside entertainment, the forest and wildlife, or visit a castle or theme park.

Caravans and motorhomes are another great way to enjoy camping. You can take all your home comforts with you, and even take extended holidays travelling long distances. Some are very small while others are luxurious; there is one to suit everyone and you can always stay in a static caravan if you prefer to stay in one location. Camping is a great family activity, so enjoy your trip!

How to use your i-SPY book

This book is arranged in sections covering different parts of the camping experience as well as things that you might do or see while you are on your trip or travelling to your campsite. As you work through the book don't forget to tick off things as you see them. You need 1000 points to send off for your i-SPY certificate (see page 64) but that is not too difficult because there are masses of points in every book. Each entry has a star or circle and points value beside it. The stars represent harder to spot entries. As you make each i-SPY, write your score in the circle or star.

Tents come in all sorts of shapes, sizes and colours. Some are supported by bendy fibreglass poles, some by metal poles and some by inflated beams. Tent material is usually nylon or cotton.

TUNNEL TENT

Points: 10

The bendy poles form a long tunnel-shaped tent with steep sides. There is plenty of room for both living and sleeping, and sometimes extended porches for cooking and storage.

Points: 10

DOME TENT

Two or more bendy poles cross over at the top to form a dome-shaped tent that is small, light and easy to pitch. The poles may be on the inside or the outside of the tent.

3

FAMILY TENT

Points: 5

These tents have enough room for up to eight people and are big enough to stand up in. They may vary in shape and design but they usually have separate compartments for sleeping and living.

Points: 20

INFLATABLE TENT

Instead of being supported by poles, these tents have inflatable tubes that are filled with air by a compressor. This makes them very quick and easy to pitch.

FRAME TENT

Points: 25

Rigid metal poles support these tents, making them very stable. They can be very heavy and take a long time to erect, so they are not as popular as they used to be.

Points: 15

15

GEODESIC TENT

Mountaineers and explorers use these tents because the series of interlocking poles creates a tent that is strong and stable but light.

RIDGE TENT

Points: 25

25

These are the classic tents. They have a straight, vertical pole at either end and a horizontal support pole across the top, forming a ridge shape. They are very stable but there is not much headroom for standing up.

TIPI

Points: 25

The traditional Native American tent is making a bit of a comeback. You can buy your own or rent one for the week at some campsites.

Points: 40   **Top Spot!**

MONGOLIAN YURT

Mongolian nomads sleep in these circular tents all year round, but you can also hire them at some campsites. The structure is made of wood or bamboo covered with insulating fur or felt to keep the living area warm.

For people who want all the fun of camping but with a few creature comforts, there are all sorts of different tents and structures to camp out in. This more glamorous form of camping is often known as 'glamping'.

Points: 25

BELL TENT

Bell tents are usually large tents with a wooden floor and some simple furnishings inside. Some of the larger ones may even have a toilet.

SAFARI TENT

Top Spot!   Points: 40

Safari tents have similar home comforts to bell tents but they are less common and so harder to spot. Usually they are hired out already erected, and make for very comfortable and relaxing camping.

Points: 30

CAMPING POD

Looking a bit like wooden tents, these pods are available to hire on some campsites. Many have carpets and electricity, making them warm and cosy to use for stays all-year-round.

As well as a tent, you need lots of extra bits and pieces to enjoy a camping trip. You'll need somewhere to sit, a stove to cook on, something to keep your food and drink cool and fresh and a nice warm sleeping bag to keep you snug and cosy at night.

CAMPING CHAIR

Points: 5

Folding chairs come in all sorts of shapes, sizes and colours. Look out for adult chairs and smaller chairs specially designed for children – often in bright colours with cool patterns!

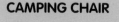 **Points: 20**

PICNIC TABLE

Campers often use a combined chair and table kit that folds up neatly to fit into the car. These are also great for taking on picnics or days out in the country.

LANTERN

Points: 10

Once night falls, you'll need something to light up the tent. Lanterns are usually battery powered and may be freestanding or hung from the roof of the tent.

FAIRY LIGHTS

These can add some extra light around the pitch and are good for helping you find your tent in the dark.

 Points: 15

AIRBED

Sleeping on the ground – even inside a sleeping bag – can be cold and uncomfortable, but you'll be much cosier if you bring an airbed along. Remember to check for leaks before you go to bed!

Points: 10

HEAD TORCH

This little device is really useful when you need to keep your hands free – great for reading and night hikes!

Points: 15

FOOTPUMP

You'll need a pump to blow up those airbeds. Take it in turns to pump or you'll get really sore legs!

 Points: 15

ELECTRIC PUMP

These make the job of pumping up the airbeds much faster. Some can be plugged into the car, otherwise you'll need an electric hook up for power.

Points: 10

SLEEPING BAG

When it's bed time, after a busy day out in the fresh air, it's great to climb inside a warm and cosy sleeping bag and curl up for the night. The best sleeping bags will even keep you warm in the depths of winter.

Points: 5

TENT PEG

These hold the tent to the ground and help to keep the tent's shape. How many can you count on one tent?

Points: 5

MALLET

No self-respecting camper would be without one. You really need one to make sure the tent pegs are firmly in the ground.

Points: 5

CITRONELLA CANDLE

Mosquitos and midges can be annoying at dusk so a citronella candle is useful for keeping them away.

Points: 20

WINDBREAK

A good windbreak is like adding an extra room to your tent and makes sitting outside much more comfortable, especially in the evenings. They are great at the beach too!

Points: 10

SOLAR LIGHT

These lights re-charge themselves during the day and are particularly handy for stopping people tripping over your guy ropes in the dark!

Points: 15

SOLAR SHOWER

Fill this black bag with water and leave it out in the sun for an hour or two. The water inside will be warm enough to shower with!

Points: 40   Top Spot!

Cooking outdoors is one of the best bits about camping. You always seem to be hungrier out in the fresh air and the food always seems to taste better. Most campers cook on a gas stove, but barbecues are also very popular and some campsites even let you cook on a proper campfire. Always take extra care around fires and cookers.

BARBECUE

Points: 10 10

Barbecues can be either gas- or charcoal-fired and are great for cooking meat and vegetables in the open air. Some are open while others have lids to keep the heat and smoky flavours in. They do get very hot though, so keep well away when they are lit.

10 **Points: 10**

GAS COOKER

This useful piece of camping kit works just like your stove at home. Don't meddle with the gas bottle though – it's very dangerous.

KETTLE

Points: 10 10

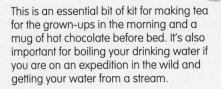

This is an essential bit of kit for making tea for the grown-ups in the morning and a mug of hot chocolate before bed. It's also important for boiling your drinking water if you are on an expedition in the wild and getting your water from a stream.

Points: 20

Some sites let you make campfires in the evening. Sitting around a glowing campfire toasting bread or marshmallows and telling spooky stories is one of the best parts of camping. Never light fires without permission and always have adults around to help.

POTS AND PANS

Points: 10

A barbecue isn't very good for cooking baked beans or pasta, so you'll need some pots and pans for cooking these on the stove.

Points: 10

COOL BOX

Milk, butter and meat all need to be kept cool in summer. The best way to keep them fresh is to take a cool box and keep it cool with freezer blocks.

FREEZER BLOCKS

Points: 10

These frozen blocks defrost very slowly in the cooler box, helping to keep food fresh. Many campsites will have a freezer where they can be frozen again.

Caravans come in many shapes and sizes, from small two berth models to massive twin wheelers. They take very little time to set up at the campsite and are just like a home-from-home.

5 **Points: 5**

SINGLE AXLE CARAVAN

Most caravans that you'll see around the site have a single axle, which means they have one set of wheels. Some are big enough to sleep up to six people.

TWIN AXLE CARAVAN

Points: 25

Larger or heavier caravans usually have two sets of wheels, making them more stable and easier to tow on the road, although they are harder to manoeuvre into place once you get to the campsite.

SWIFT

Points: 10

Swift are a British caravan manufacturer who make three ranges of caravan: Swift, Sprite and Sterling, each with several different models. Score for any of the three ranges you see.

Points: 10

BAILEY

Bailey are a very popular British caravan maker who have produced several different models over the years such as the Pegasus, which uses new caravan technology to make it very strong.

LUNAR

Points: 10

Lunar is another make of caravan you are almost certain to see on any caravan site. The company name was inspired by the first landing on the moon!

Points: 50   Top Spot!

TEARDROP TRAILER

There isn't room for much more than a bed in these tiny caravans, but some have basic cooking facilities, a fridge and a small sink or water storage all stored in the rear. They can be towed by a small car. If you don't need all of the luxuries of a full size caravan but you want something that can be moved to a new location at a moment's notice, this will do the job.

AIRSTREAM TRAILER

Top Spot!   **Points: 40**   40

These caravans originate from America where the first factory opened in Culver City, California in 1931. Their distinctive rounded shape and shiny polished aluminium exterior add a touch of glamour to the campsite. The largest models can sleep 8 people.

15   **Points: 15**

STATIC CARAVAN

Some campsites have a few static caravans available for hire. They are bigger and more luxurious than touring caravans and have separate rooms inside them.

Modern caravans are warm and comfortable with many appliances and gadgets. Inside you will find bedroom, kitchen and living areas and often a separate bathroom - just like at home but a lot smaller.

Points: 5

LOUNGE

Most caravans have a lounge area that turns into a bedroom at night. You simply pull out some wooden slats between the settees, rearrange the cushions and you have a big, comfy bed.

FIXED BED

Points: 15

Many caravans include a fixed bed. It takes a lot of space, but there's usually room to store things underneath and you get a really good night's sleep.

Points: 15

BUNK BEDS

Lots of caravans have bunk beds specially designed for children to sleep in. These bunks are quite comfy and some have their own lights, windows and curtains.

MICROWAVE

Most caravans have microwaves fitted into their kitchens. They're ideal for cooking tea when it's raining and too wet for a barbecue outside.

 Points: 15

FRIDGE

All but the smallest caravans have their own fridge, which are powered by mains electricity, a big battery or gas. They keep food and drink cool and fresh, but they don't usually have as much room as your fridge at home.

Points: 5

SHOWER

Many caravans have hot and cold running water, so if you've had a hard day exploring, you can enjoy a nice warm shower in your own caravan – just don't forget to close the cubicle, or you'll get water everywhere!

 Points: 10

TELEVISION

Small televisions are ideal for caravans. Some have built-in DVD players, so you can watch films on rainy days.

Points: 10
double with DVD player

As well as a caravan, there are lots of other things you might need to go caravanning. See how many of these caravan accessories you can spot around the campsite.

(5) **Points: 5**

GAS BOTTLE

Caravans need gas for heating, cooking and in some cases, to power the fridge. The bottles are usually stored in a special locker at the front of the caravan behind the towing hitch.

WATER CONTAINER

Points: 10 **(10)**

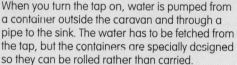

When you turn the tap on, water is pumped from a container outside the caravan and through a pipe to the sink. The water has to be fetched from the tap, but the containers are specially designed so they can be rolled rather than carried.

(10) **Points: 10**

ELECTRIC HOOK-UP

The vast majority of sites now provide electric hook-up (EHU) points for caravans and tents. These provide mains electricity to power everything from the toaster to the telly. Some EHU points have meters to measure the amount of electricity used.

AWNING

Points: 15

Awnings give caravanners a lot of extra space for living or storage. There might be a full awning, which runs almost the entire length of the caravan, or a porch awning, which just surrounds the door.

 Points: 5

HITCH AND STABILISER

All caravans need a hitch to hook on to the car's towbar so they can be towed. The stabiliser stops the caravan snaking from side to side when being towed.

WASTE WATER CONTAINER

Points: 10

Water drains from the sink into this container, which has wheels for when you take it to the grey water disposal point for emptying.

Motorhomes are like vans with a caravan on the back and they are becoming more and more popular in the UK. They range in size from tiny little micro campers based on compact delivery vans right up to huge luxury versions based on a bus chassis. See how many different sorts you can spot – both on the road and on a campsite.

Points: 25

MICRO CAMPER

These compact little motorhomes are popular with people who are keen on outdoor sports, but want something a little bit more luxurious than a tent. The roof may lift up to create extra headroom and there's a sink, gas hob and sometimes even a toilet on board.

CAMPER VAN

Points: 15

Campers are great for days out, weekends away and even short holidays in the summer. Life is a bit cramped on board, but they have beds, a small kitchen and sometimes even a toilet. Look out for classic Volkswagen campers with funky paintwork.

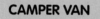

Martin Charles Hatch / Shutterstock.com

VAN CONVERSION

Points: 20

This kind of motorhome is converted from a delivery van such as a Ford Transit or Fiat Ducato. Modern construction techniques are making them more and more luxurious, with a kitchen, toilet, beds and a compact bathroom all crammed inside.

Points: 25

COACHBUILT MOTORHOME

Coachbuilt motorhomes use a van chassis with a separate living compartment fixed onto it. They generally have more space than campers or van conversions and can be up to 8 metres long, with some having a twin axle at the rear.

40 Points: 40 Top Spot!

LUXURY LINER

The biggest and most expensive motorhomes are often called 'liners'. These luxurious vehicles have all the appliances and gadgets you'll ever need, but they can cost more than a house!

VIP TOURBUS

Top Spot! Points: 50 **50**

Look out for luxury liners with tinted windows - there might be a celebrity on board! Singers and bands sometimes travel in VIP tourbuses if they are travelling for long distances but don't want to fly. They are also handy for transporting instruments.

You might have a long journey to make before you reach your campsite. See if you can spot some of these things along the way to help pass the time.

CAR WITH BIKES

Points: 10

CAR WITH BOAT

Leonard Zhukovsky / Shutterstock.com

Points: 25
double for a boat on a trailer

ROOFBOX

JuliusKielaitis / Shutterstock.com

Points: 10

HORSEBOX

Points: 25

Points: 20
2 Lanes: 30; 3 Lanes or more: 50

If you're waiting to drive onto the ferry, all the caravans will usually park up in the same queue. Count how many lanes are full of caravans.

AT THE GARAGE

Points: 15

Look out for caravans and motorhomes at filling stations. Caravans need a lot of room to manoeuvre, so most caravanners try to fill up before they hitch up the caravan. Get 15 points if you spot a caravan or motorhome filling up at a garage.

Points: 10

CAMPSITE SIGN

Will you be the first to spot a sign to your campsite?

DIFFERENT SITES

Britain has thousands of campsites and there are even more on the continent. Campsites can be little more than a field with a tap in the corner or a fantastic holiday complex with heated swimming pools, cafés, restaurants and bars. Which type will you stay on?

CLUB SITE

Points: 25

Some of the best sites in Britain belong to clubs, although non-members can usually stay as well. They are well run with good facilities.

Points: 10

COASTAL SITE

If you're really lucky, you could stay on a site right next to the beach!

HOLIDAY COMPLEX

Points: 20

These big complexes are great for families, because there's always something going on whatever the weather.

Points: 30

FOREST SITE

Camping in the forest feels very different to being in an open field. Listen out for the sounds of nature at night.

FARM SITE

Points: 20

Many farmers turn part of their working farm into a campsite. If you're lucky you may get the chance to have a look around the farm. What kind of farm are you staying on?

RALLY SITE

Top Spot!   Points: 40

Meeting up with other people who share a particular interest can be a good way to make new friends. Rally sites are often temporary campsites on playing fields or even on school fields.

Points: 40   Top Spot!

FESTIVAL SITE

You can really make the most of a festival by camping on the site. With so many people around it can get very muddy when it rains, so don't forget your wellies!

Jason Batterham / Shutterstock.com

There are lots of things to see around the campsite. The type of facilities will depend on how big it is and whether there are caravans, motorhomes, holiday homes or just tents.

5 **Points: 5**

RECEPTION

Most sites have a reception building somewhere near the main entrance. This is where you check in. Sometimes it has a little shop selling camping essentials (like ice cream!). The helpful people at the reception desk will answer any questions you have.

UNLOADING THE CAR

Points: 5 **5**

Once you've arrived at the campsite, there's usually a lot of unloading to be done – especially if you are staying in a tent. A roofbox provides extra space for carrying all those important extras.

TOILET BLOCK

All but the smallest sites will have a toilet block where you'll find separate toilets and showers. More and more sites are installing solar panels to heat the water in their shower blocks.

 Points: 10

SWIMMING POOL

Holiday Complex sites often have a swimming pool. This may be inside or outside – some even have both so you can swim whatever the weather!

Points: 25

POT WASH

It's really handy to have a proper sink with hot running water to do the washing up in. These can be either inside or outside.

Points: 10

INFORMATION HUT

Some sites have a tourist information hut with maps and leaflets of places to visit during your stay.

Points: 20

Points: 25

LAUNDRY

Larger campsites will have a laundry with washing machines and sinks where clothes can be washed and dried. Very useful if you're staying for a long time or if you get muddy while you're out

CHEMICAL TOILET DISPOSAL

Points: 15

Caravan and camper van toilets have a cassette which needs to be emptied into the campsite's sewage system. There are special points where this can be done hygienically.

Points: 5

WATER TAP

All campsites will have a tap where you can get fresh water for drinking and cooking.

MOWER

Points: 15

There is usually a lot of grass on the campsite, which needs regular mowing during the summer months. Ride on mowers get the job done quickly.

5 **Points: 5**

DOG

Camping is great for dogs because they love to be outdoors. They need to be kept on a lead around the campsite in case they run away.

There are plenty of things to do inside and outside while on holiday. If it's dry and sunny, a lot of people eat outside. But don't worry if it rains; a cosy caravan lounge is a great place to play board games and read your favourite book.

Points: 10

CYCLING

Taking a bike is a great way of getting around the campsite and exploring the surrounding countryside.

FISHING

Points: 15

Lots of campsites are near lakes or rivers. Some are almost close enough to let you fish from your tent!

OUTDOOR GAMES

Points: 10 (10)

Frisbee, swingball and soft tennis are great games for the campsite, or if it isn't too windy you could also play badminton.

(10) **Points: 10**

INDOOR GAMES

urbanbuzz / Shutterstock.com

When it's wet outside, the best place to be is around the table for some family games. Score for any board game!

EAT OUTSIDE

Points: 10 (10)

You'll probably see lots of people eating outside if it's sunny. Breakfast outdoors is a great way to start your day – especially with a few rashers of bacon sizzling away on the barbecue. Mmm!

Points: 20

SAIL IN A DINGHY

Taking a rubber dinghy on a camping expedition gives you the chance to explore any lakes or rivers near the campsite – and it will help you stay cool in summer. Just remember to always wear a life-jacket.

PONY TREKKING

 Points: 25

There are many riding stables that will organise a pony trek for people of all abilities. It's a great way to see the countryside.

Points: 10

HIKING

There are some beautiful views on the paths through the British countryside. Hiking is a great way to explore them whilst camping – just make sure you take some snacks and water, and a map so you do not get lost!

FOSSIL HUNTING

Top Spot!   Points: 40   40

You may be lucky enough to find prehistoric creatures or plants preserved in rocks on the coast or hillside, giving a glimpse of how the environment was millions of years ago. This is a fossil ammonite, you can see the spiral shape of the shell. Ammonites lived between 65 and 240 million years ago and became extinct around the same time as the dinosaurs.

Points: 20

TOAST MARSHMALLOWS

A real camping tradition! Spear a marshallow onto a skewer and hold it over the campfire to toast! There's nothing like the taste of hot, gooey marshmallows. Just be careful – campfires can be dangerous.

GO CRABBING

Points: 25

You will find crabs in rock pools at low tide, or by catching them with a line from a pier or harbour wall using cooked ham as bait. Remember to return them to the water afterwards.

Points: 10

GO ON A NIGHT HIKE

Going for a walk after dark can be great fun. Look out for nocturnal animals such as hedgehogs, bats and owls and don't forget to take a torch!

When you visit a area, it's fun to go out and about and discover new places to see. There are so many visitor attractions around and about that there is never enough time to see them all!

BEACH

If your campsite is near the seaside, you'll be able to spend lots of time on the beach. Some sites are so close to the sea that you can walk straight from your caravan or tent to the beach.

 **Points: 25**

VISIT A CASTLE

There are lots of castles to visit around the country. Some are in ruins while others have been preserved, but they all have interesting histories.

Points: 25

ANIMAL PARK

Zoos, animal sanctuaries and wildlife parks are great places to get up close to lots of different animal species and learn more about them.

CIRCUS

Points: 35

If you are lucky there might be a circus near your campsite. Go and watch talented performers as you nibble on candy floss and popcorn.

THEME PARK

Points: 30

Thrill-seekers will enjoy a day at a theme park, although there are usually gentler rides too and often other attractions like zoos and 4D cinemas.

Points: 40 **Top Spot!**

MUSIC FESTIVAL

Music festivals range from huge gatherings like Glastonbury, where famous bands perform live on stage, to much smaller events designed to appeal more to families. There might be craft workshops, storytelling and theatre. Write down who you saw perform here: ....
....
....

Points: 40   Top Spot!

Also called County Shows, they have displays of massive farm machinery and marquees full of blow-dried and brushed farm animals all looking their best as their owners hope for a rosette from the judge.

MINIATURE RAILWAY

Points: 25

You will find miniature railways all around the country, often in parks, at the seaside and in zoos. Many of them are pulled by steam locomotives.

Points: 25

BOAT TRIP

Take a boat trip on a lake, down a canal or on the sea. You could travel to an island or go wildlife spotting.

Our nation is criss-crossed with a multitude of footpaths where you can take in the views and spot wildlife while you walk. These paths could take you along the coast, through the woods, beside a river or across farmers' fields.

Points: 10

FOOTPATH SIGN

Public rights of way are denoted by signs like this one, which show that you have a right to walk along the footpath.

STILE

Points: 20

A simple but clever design built in a wall or hedge that allows the easy passage of walkers but not the livestock.

Points: 30

BRIDLEWAY

Horses can be ridden along these paths, which can usually be used by walkers and cyclists too.

FOOTBRIDGE

Points: 25

Footbridges may be made of wood, metal or stone and they allow us to cross rivers, roads, railways and canals. Remember to stop and play pooh sticks if you're crossing a river.

Points: 15

HEDGEROW

These are planted along field boundaries and beside paths and are great for wildlife. Look out for birds and insects among the shrubs.

46

Points: 20

DRY STONE WALL

These are skilfully made by stacking stones together without the use of mortar. They are very effective and often last for centuries.

FARMER'S FIELD

Points: 10
double for a tractor too

The countryside is covered with farmers' fields, some containing livestock such as cows or sheep, and others used for growing crops. Score extra points if there's a tractor in the field too.

Points: 10

Waterfalls occur as, over time, a stream of water flows over hard and onto softer rock. The softer material is eroded by the water as it flows downhill. The waterfall with the tallest single drop in Britain at 200 m (658 ft) is called Eas a' Chual Aluinn. It is in a remote part of northern Scotland.

Points: 15

MOUNTAIN STREAM

Rain falls on to rocky mountain slopes and naturally runs downhill. It collects numerous tiny trickles along the way and eventually becomes a fast flowing stream and then a river.

On a sunny day what better thing to do than have a day out to the seaside. There are beaches and resorts all around the UK coast with plenty of things to enjoy.

5 **Points: 5**

BEACH TENT

These handy little tents take just a few minutes to erect. They provide a sand free place for the sandwiches and shelter to keep the drinks cool too. They can even be used to change in.

BEACHCOMBING

Points: 15 **15**

Shells of all sizes and colours can be found on the beach. Sometimes people use metal detectors to find more valuable items such as jewellery or coins.

ROCKPOOLING

Points: 15

Rockpool water is generally crystal clear. If you are patient little fish, crabs and shrimps will come out of hiding. The best pools to look in are close to the sea. Move seaweed or rocks to get a better view and take a net and a bucket so you can look at creatures for a while before putting them back.

Points: 20

WALKING ON THE PIER

The first pleasure pier was built in England in 1813 and people have been enjoying them ever since. Today a pier may contain food stalls, gaming arcades, and even a theatre.

15 **Points: 15**

AMUSEMENT ARCADE

No seaside would be complete without an amusement arcade. Slot machines and teddy pickers are great fun but be careful how much money you spend!

CAROUSEL

Points: 20

Also known as merry-go-rounds, these fairground rides often play music as you go round and round and up and down on the horse.

FLYING A KITE

Points: 25

They don't take up much space in the tent or caravan and even a basic kite can be made to dance across the sky. With a little practise you can make specialized kites do amazing stunts.

Points: 5

FISH AND CHIPS

Nothing tastes quite as good as fish and chips on the beach! It's Britain's favourite seaside meal.

10 Points: 10

SURFING/BODYBOARDING

Many beaches are well known for their surf waves. A wetsuit means that you can surf or board most times of the year.

SANDCASTLE

Points: 5 **5**

Everyone loves a sandcastle. Who cares if your clothes get a little damp and a bit sandy, they can always be shaken out later.

SAND SCULPTURE

Points: 10

If you see a sand artist on the beach, stop and watch for a while. You may learn some new techniques that you can use to create your own masterpiece later in the day. Some beaches hold competitions and award prizes for the best sand scultures. Write down what you saw built as a sand sculpture here:.............. ....

Nature is all around us and you won't have to go far to find it. See what you can find on your campsite, and look out for some of these plants and animals when you are out and about.

Points: 10

BEECH AND BEECHMAST

Beech trees have traditionally been used to make furniture, and the off cuts make excellent firewood. Beechmast (nuts) are harvested by many wild creatures including squirrels, wild boar and deer as well as a number of different birds.

YEW AND YEW SEED CAP

Points: 10

The yew is a member of the conifer family. It is slow growing and can live for thousands of years. Seed is stored inside a red berry and sought out by members of the thrush family. Parts of the tree are used to make a medicine to fight cancer.

HAZEL AND HAZELNUT

Points: 10

Catkins on a hazel tree are a good indication that spring is on the way. The ripened hazelnuts are a valuable source of winter food for jays, squirrels and dormice.

Points: 10

ENGLISH OAK AND ACORN

The wood from the mighty oak is strong and has been used for centuries in house building, shipbuilding and for making storage barrels. The bark of the oak tree contains tannin which is used in preserving and tanning leather.

COMMON ASH AND ASH KEYS

Points: 10

Ash wood can easily be bent when heated with steam and is often used to make handles for tools, sports equipment, furniture and even walking sticks.

Points: 10

This is probably the first tree that children learn to recognise. Why? The seeds of the tree are better known as conkers and are great to play with. Conkers start out round and green – you know they are strong enough to play with when their green case becomes sharp and spiky.

RAGWORT

Points: 10

This plant, which has bright yellow flowers, is a member of the daisy family. Althought it's pretty to look at, it's very poisonous to humans and animals.

Points: 10

WOODBINE

This deciduous climber is the wild version of honeysuckle. It produces a heavenly scent, mainly at night, to attract pollinating insects and produces bright red berries in autumn.

CREEPING BUTTERCUP

Points: 5 5

Beautiful to look at, the buttercup spreads quickly by sending out several runners, each with a baby plant on the end, which send down roots and start the cycle again.

5 **Points: 5**

DOG ROSE

The dog rose has pale pink flowers in summer and in autumn produces bright red hips which contain highly beneficial levels of vitamin C and can be made into a medicinal syrup.

Points: 10

These fluffy cottonwool clouds change shape as they move across the sky. What shapes can you see in them?

RAINBOW

Points: 20
double points for a double rainbow

If the sun comes out during a rain shower, the light is refracted and dispersed by the water droplets to form this beautiful coloured arch in the sky.

Points: 35

THUNDER AND LIGHTNING

Thunder storms can be very loud when you are camping! Look out for forked lightning, but remember to keep safe.

HARBOUR PORPOISE

Top Spot! **Points: 50**

Porpoises are cetaceans that can be seen in the shallow coastal waters around Britain. You will usually only see the dark grey arch of their backs and the small triangular dorsal fin as they swim close to the surface of the water.

Points: 20

BAT

These flying mammals come out after sunset during the summer months. You may see them quickly darting around as they pluck insects from the air or water.

Points: 5

ROBIN

Robins are present in the UK all year round. You may well see them on the campsite, especially if you leave some birdseed on the ground for them.

OYSTERCATCHER

Points: 10

These birds are found on the coast, often in groups. They are very striking as they scurry about the beach and rocks looking for shellfish, though they prefer to eat mussels than oysters.

Points: 5   5

You are more likely to see a wild rabbit early in the morning or in the evening. They live in family groups in underground burrows and feed on grass and weeds.

INDEX

i-SPY

How to get your i-SPY certificate and badge

Let us know when you've become a super-spotter with 1000 points and we'll send you a special certificate and badge!

HERE'S WHAT TO DO!

- ✓ Ask an adult to check your score.

- ✓ Visit www.collins.co.uk/i-SPY to apply for your certificate. If you are under the age of 13 you will need a parent or guardian to do this.

- ✓ We'll send your certificate via email and you'll receive a brilliant badge through the post!